TOOL BOOKLET

—

Maintaining Your Breakthrough

© Copyright 2014 Barry and Lori Byrne
www.nothinghidden.com

ISBN 978-1-941218-10-5
January 2015 Edition

All rights reserved. This book and it's material is protected by the copyright laws of the United States of America. This book may not be copied or reprinted for commercial gain or profit. The use of short quotations or occasional page copying for personal or group study only is permitted. Permission will be granted upon request. Unless otherwise identified, Scripture quotations are from the New American Standard Bible®, used by permission.

Copyright © 1960, 1962, 1963, 1968, 1971, 1972, 1973, 1975, 1977, 1995 by The Lockman Foundation. (lockman.org)

Dear Nothing Hidden Ministries Participants,

God has given us many ways to strengthen marriages, transform individual lives, and equip leaders to mentor others through the workshops of Nothing Hidden Ministries.

Regularly practicing the "tools" is one of the best ways to develop your confidence to overcome the obstacles that come against you, your relationships or your marriage. It is the practicing on your own that builds confidence in the Lord's readiness to take your simple, consistent efforts and make your victories sure.

In order to help you accomplish this goal, we have compiled all the tools from Love After Marriage and Single Life Workshop in one booklet for quick reference and for easy use. Our prayer is that you will join the army of overcomers who know their God's ability to deliver them, and then become a part of those used to strengthen and raise up marriage and Godly relationships to its rightful place in the Body of Christ and in the world.

With Great Affection,
Barry & Lori Byrne

CONTENTS

RULES FOR SHARING	1
LISTENING EXERCISE	2
FEELING WORDS	4
GENERATIONAL PRAYER	5
FORGIVENESS TOOL	6
BREAKING VOWS AND CURSES	9
BREAKING SOUL TIES	10
1-2-3 SKIDOO!	11
THE SPIRITUAL WEAPON OF CONFESSION	12
SPIRITUAL WEAPONS FOR OVERCOMERS	14
WHEN THE POOP HITS THE FAN	16
SPIRIT BLESSING	17
STEPS TO RECONCILIATION	20
RULES FOR WORKING THROUGH CONFLICT	21
REVEAL YOUR MIND EXERCISE	24
GODLY GRIEVING	25

SPECIFIC TOOLS FOR MARRIED COUPLES

IDEAS FOR GOING DEEPER	28
THE 4-2 MAINTENANCE PLAN	29
CEREMONY OF LOVING COMMITMENT	30

RULES FOR SHARING

1. When one person is talking, everyone *really* listens.

2. When a couple or an individual is sharing, questions need to be limited to:

    Clarification: "I didn't understand that."
    "Could you repeat that?"

    More information: "Could you explain why?"
    "How did you feel when that happened?"

3. When asked to give feedback to the person sharing, with a spouse a friend or in a small group:

    Always start with what you can affirm and agree with; *then* share other opinions or questions.

    In all your responses, be thinking of how to build this person up and encourage them with what God has for them.

4. **Confidentiality for group sharing:**

    Commit to respecting the vulnerability and trust given to you during any open and honest sharing.

LISTENING EXERCISE

The purpose of this exercise is simply to connect with each other by understanding the other person's words and feelings. When responding to your spouse or the other person, try to use individual feeling words as much as possible rather than long, wordy explanations. No fixing problems or giving advice is allowed. There is a time for problem solving but for the sake of learning this tool, this is not it!

Also, for the sake of learning this tool, please use non-volatile issues. Don't bring up unresolved problems in your marriage or relationship.

1. **One person briefly describes one part of an issue, 10-20 seconds maximum.**

    Talk about something of importance to you that is unresolved. It could be about work, family or any other situation or issue of significance to you.

The second person listens for what the first person is *saying* and *feeling*.

- After the first person talks, your job is to respond with words that let them know you understand them, what they are feeling, and why this is important to them. There are feeling words on the next page if needed.

- Once you have responded, ask for feedback to find out how closely you understood the first person.

- If you did well, the first person should let you know that they felt understood by you. If you did not understand well, ask for more explanation (10-20 seconds maximum) and try responding again.

- Continue this process until the first person can say, "Yes, you understand me and know how I'm feeling."

- Do not let offense in if it takes you several tries! Remember this is about understanding them, not about you getting it wrong or right.

2. **Second person, ask the first person to let you know how it felt to be listened to and understood.**

FEELING WORDS

AFFECTIONATE
close
loving
passionate
sexy
tender

AFRAID
apprehensive
fearful
frightened
horrified
nervous
petrified
scared
terrified
threatened

ANGRY
annoyed
bitter
enraged
frustrated
furious
hateful
indignant
infuriated
irate
irritated
livid
offended
enraged
ticked off

DOUBTFUL
defeated
distrustful
dubious
helpless
hesitant
hopeless
powerless
skeptical
unsettled

EAGER
anxious
enthusiastic
excited

FEARLESS
bold
brave
courageous
daring
determined

HURT
aching
afflicted
betrayed
crushed
distressed

HAPPY
amused
carefree
cheerful
delighted
ecstatic
elated
excited
exhilarated
joyful
playful

INTERESTED
curious
excited
fascinated
intrigued

SAD
choked up
disappointed
discouraged
heavy-hearted
low
sorrowful
unhappy

GENERATIONAL PRAYER

I place the cross of Jesus in my family bloodline (repeat)
And I sever all ties (repeat)
With this ungodly part of my natural heritage (repeat)
That has manifested (repeat)
(Name the things the Lord has shown you that have come against you.)

I claim the power of the cross (repeat)
All generations back and all generations forward (repeat)
To break the power of all the demonic spirits assigned to me (repeat)
To perpetuate this in my family line (repeat)

By the power of the cross (repeat)
In the name of Jesus Christ (repeat)
I command these demonic spirits and lies: (repeat)
Out of my life (repeat)
Out of my thoughts (repeat)
Out of my perceptions of myself and others (repeat)
Out of my feelings and emotions (repeat)
Out of my relationships (repeat)
Out of my ways of relating to others (repeat)
Away from my marriage or potential marriage (repeat)
Away from my children or potential children (repeat)
Out of my/our destiny and calling (repeat)
And completely out of my/our future (repeat)

I seal this in my spirit in the name of Jesus!

FORGIVENESS TOOL

This tool is an aide in helping you lead yourself or another person through forgiveness. If you're leading another person, have them participate with you in adding things that they need to forgive.

True forgiveness goes beyond simply forgiving someone for their behavior and the wrong they did. Forgiveness involves forgiving someone for all of the hurt and pain they have caused, as well as the effects of those hurts in your life.

Count on Holy Spirit releasing prophetic words and discernment to you beyond your own understanding. Step out, take a risk and watch what Holy Spirit will do with these steps:

1. **Father God, thank you for forgiving me for all my sins. Because of your forgiveness, I also forgive (person's name).**

2. **(Person's name), I forgive you for the lies the enemy brought to me as a result of your actions or words.**

   Listen to Holy Spirit and say the lies as they come in each of these categories below:

   Lies about:
   … Myself… (name the lies about yourself)
   … My relationships… (name the lies about your relationships)
   … My view of men/women… (name the lies about this)
   … My view of marriage… (name the lies about marriage)
   … My view of motherhood/fatherhood… (name the lies here)
   … My view of God… (name the lies about God)
   … (Other)… (name any other lies)

3. **(Person's name), I forgive you for bringing fear into my life.**
   (For example: Fear of intimacy, failure, being alone, death, not being enough, fear of man… these are just some examples. Listen to what Holy Spirit is saying about this situation.)

   Fear of _____
   Fear of _____
   Fear of _____ …, etc.

4. **(Person's name), I forgive you for opening the door to:**
   (For example: Anger, self-hatred, passivity, accusation, feelings of worthlessness, shame, self-protection, sexual perversion, shutting down, depression, the occult... these are just some examples. Listen to what Holy Spirit is saying about this situation.)

   Opening the door to _____
   Opening the door to _____
   Opening the door to _____ ..., etc.

5. **(Person's name), I forgive you for the lack of:** *(For example: Protection, love, nurturing, relationship, knowing me, affection, attention, care, stability, etc... these are just some examples. Listen to what Holy Spirit is saying about this situation.)*

   Lack of _____
   Lack of _____
   Lack of _____ ..., etc.

6. **(Person's name), I forgive you for all of the pain and suffering that I've had to deal with [throughout my life] because of what you did.**

7. **Pray and bless the person that you just forgave.**

(See Forgiveness Tool example on the next page.)

This is an example of what it might look like to go through this Forgiveness Tool: *A woman was sexually abused by her father as a young girl. Below is an example of what forgiving her father might look like:*

Father God, thank you for forgiving me of all my sins. Because of your forgiveness, I also forgive you, Dad.
Dad, I forgive you for being the perpetrator and not my protector.
I forgive you for not knowing me or caring about me in the ways I needed.
I forgive you for bringing me a bad example of what a father is, causing me to fear and mistrust you.
I forgive you for causing me to mistrust and even hate men.
I forgive you for misrepresenting God to me.
I forgive you for making me not want Him.
I forgive you for making me feel dirty and like I'm damaged goods.
I forgive you for making me shut down emotionally.
I forgive you for causing me trouble in my marriage because I see my husband like I've seen you.
I forgive you for not loving and cherishing my mother.
I forgive you for giving me such a skewed view of marriage.
I forgive you for making me afraid of intimacy."

Note: At times, when people are working through painful life experiences and invite Jesus into a memory, they are still unable to see Jesus in the memory or they see a counterfeit "false Jesus" who is detached, standing in the doorway with arms folded, aloof, judgmental and distant (all things that Jesus would never be or do). Forgiveness is one of the tools that will open the door for them to see the real Jesus.

BREAKING VOWS AND CURSES

Vows: Most of the time these are made unknowingly and often times when we were young during hardship, fear, crisis, trauma, abuse, disappointment... (For example, someone might have said, "I will avoid disappointment at all cost.")

Curses: Destructive words that you or others have spoken over yourself. (For example, "I'm such a loser.")

Use 1-2-3 Skidoo! or Generational Prayer to break vows and curses.

Examples:

Vows:
- I will never let myself need anyone.
- I will always have to be my own protector.
- I cannot trust women/men.
- I will never cry again.
- I will always make sure everyone is happy, no matter what it takes.

Curses:
- You are such an idiot!
- You'll never amount to anything.
- I wish you were more like your brother.
- You don't have the intelligence to go to college.
- Can't you do anything right?!

BREAKING SOUL TIES

Bless your spirit to lead your soul and body and connect with Holy Spirit as He leads you into all truth.

In the name of Jesus, I break the power of all ungodly spirit, soul and bodily ties forged between _____ and me.

By the power of the cross, I send back to _____ all parts of him/her that he/she gave to me.

And I take back from _____ all parts of me that I gave to him/her.

Father, I ask you to set a guard over my spirit, soul and body to never again connect with _____ in this ungodly way.

I nail to the cross the lie that joining with _____ was necessary, needed or wanted.

I break all agreements I've made with this lie known or unknown and I turn away from joining with it.

Father, as you send this lie away from me, what is the truth about this situation you want me to know?

1-2-3 SKIDOO!

Talk about what is coming against you and what it is trying to steal from you. You may be able to do this on your own or you may need help from your spouse or a close friend whom you trust.

As the thoughts come that are not from God, you must catch them. You must not allow them to just go through your mind. Take them captive using these three simple steps:

1. I nail _____ to the cross.

    The thoughts could come as a feeling (anger, depression, hopelessness, rejection, self-protection, etc). They could also come as words or thoughts you're hearing like, "He doesn't really care about me," or "She's never going to change."

    You can even say, "'She's never going to change,' I nail you to the cross."

    Or… "Depression, I nail you to the cross!"

2. I break all agreements I've made with _____ known or unknown and I repent of joining with _____.

3. I ask You, Father, to send _____ away from me!

    Father, what do You want to give me in place of _____?

THE SPIRITUAL WEAPON OF CONFESSION

Confession: From a Greek word meaning *"to speak the same,"* also meaning to *"assent,"* that is to consider something carefully and then to come into agreement.

Confession to God is the process of thinking through things carefully until we come to the place where we think and speak the same as what God thinks and speaks about us and our situation.

Confession is a much larger concept than simply admitting when we have done something wrong. Confession and repentance are necessary after we have sinned; however, confession is a powerful spiritual weapon to use against sin when it comes to us in the form of temptation. When sin comes to us to tempt us into sinning, sincere confession puts God to work on our behalf to send away the sin according to I John 1:9.

Tools to help us get our thoughts and our words in alignment with God:

1. Ask yourself the question, *"What would Jesus say about me and my situation?"*

    Based on what Jesus said about Himself, His nature and character, and how He interacted with people, what would He say to me about me and my situation?

2. Answer the following questions from God's perspective as though God were speaking to you:

    What effect is this _____ having on my relationship to God?
    What effect is this _____ having on the fruit of the Spirit in me?
    How does this _____ make me feel about myself?
    What effect is this _____ having on my relationships to those that are closest to me?
    What good thing that God wants me to have in my life is this _____ trying to steal, kill or destroy?

(Continued on the next page)

3. Make sure that your answers agree with the Word of God from the Bible and His heart of compassion towards us.

4. Now declare the answers that God has given you for the five questions above.

   Now, continue confessing and declaring the answers to these questions whenever needed. If you are finding and speaking what God would speak, you are speaking the truth. God and all of Heaven will support the truth.

   Confess and declare the truth no matter how you feel. If you will persist in this process, eventually your mind and your heart will come into agreement with God's truth.

5. Confession requires a simultaneous commitment to obedience or the confession is merely meaningless words that will result in an unstable life.

   As you persist in this process, you will mature and you will become better trained to discern good and evil.
   (Matthew 7:21-27; Hebrews 5:11-14; John 7:17; 8:31, 32)

SPIRITUAL WEAPONS FOR OVERCOMERS

I CONFESS the work of sin coming against me.
Confession is carefully considering my situation and bringing my thoughts and words about this issue into agreement with God. Sin is missing the mark so as not to share in the prize. Sin is anything that keeps me from having the good things that God wants to give me. Talk to God in detail about the good things that sin is attempting to steal or destroy in your life. **(I John 1:9; Romans 7:17, 20)**

I REPENT and ask Your forgiveness for any way I have participated in that sin.

Note: It is important to distinguish between sin that comes as temptation which must be resisted and sin that you participate in which requires repentance and forgiveness. **(I Peter 5:8-9; Hebrews 12:4; Acts 3:14)**

I nail _____ to the CROSS OF JESUS CHRIST where You overcame and condemned all sin, death and darkness.
Thank you, Jesus, that you have given me your Spirit to enable me to overcome this as you did. **(Colossians 2:13-15; Galatians 6:14; I Peter 2:24)**

In the NAME OF JESUS, I tell _____ to leave me.
Get away from me and stay away in Jesus' name. **(Mark 16:17; Acts 4:7)**

I ask you, Jesus, to CLEANSE ME WITH YOUR BLOOD.
I receive the power of Your pure, spotless blood that was shed for me. Cleanse my mind and my heart so that I can see myself and my situation the same as You see it. **(I John 1:7; Revelation 12:10-11; I Corinthians 2:16)**

(Continued on the next page)

HOLY SPIRIT, PLEASE FILL ME with your spirit of _____
instead of _____ .

For example, instead of anger, Jesus wants to fill you with the fruit of His Spirit, patience, gentleness and kindness. Instead of a spirit of fear, Jesus wants you to have power, love and a sound mind. He wants you to know His perfect love that casts out all fear. Instead of worry, He wants you to have His peace rule. Instead of agreeing with false accusation about yourself, ask Him to fill you with His spirit of truth, etc.
(I John 1:7; I Peter 5:6-11; Luke 8:18; John 17:17; II Timothy 1:7)

THANK GOD that He will make you stronger as you trust Him through this difficulty. **(Romans 5:3-5; I Thessalonians 5:18; James 1:2-4)**

WORSHIP AND PRAISE God for His power to enable you to overcome anything that the enemy brings to you. **(I Corinthians 10:13; Romans 8:36, 37)**

WHEN THE POOP HITS THE FAN

A Godly option to deal with "stuff" in the heat of the moment.

1. **Choose not to leave.** If you must leave to cool down or get control of your tongue, tell your spouse or the other person what you're doing and that you will be back. If it is longer than five minutes, give them a time when you will come back to talk. Stay in the battle. If you are tempted to physically leave or emotionally withdraw or shut down–*don't*!

2. **Stand back to back.** Ask Jesus to come as the Wonderful Counselor and pray in tongues or English for a few minutes until you feel a slight shift in your spirit or emotions.

3. **Remain standing.** Take turns nailing to the cross whatever you're feeling that is not from God. Break agreements with it and ask the Father to send it away–out loud!

    Example:
    "In the name of Jesus, I nail (anger, frustration, separation, accusation, fear, rejection) to the cross of Jesus."
    "I break all agreements I've made with it."
    "I ask You, Father, to send away from me."

4. **Now turn and face one another, holding hands (if you are married).** Discuss the issues respectfully, not joining with accusation and anger, etc.

5. **If discussion is going well, finish.** But if not, stop and declare the truth about what you are dealing with. Start with overall truths about yourself and your marriage or relationship. Then get specific. Don't rush this.

6. **If either spouse/person needs to ask forgiveness, do so.**

SPIRIT BLESSING

We have seen the Lord use this very simple tool of blessing (by Arthur Burk) to legitimize each other's spirits in wonderful ways. As couples bless each other's spirits to lead their souls and bodies, they often experience intimate connection and dramatic changes. Singles, parents and children, even teachers and students have used Sprit Blessing to nurture each other's spirits resulting in significant breakthroughs. Do not under estimate this tool! The Lord has really been highlighting this. There is an anointing on it for breakthrough!

SPIRIT BLESSING FOR COUPLES

Morning & Night Blessings

1. **Bless your own spirit or your spouse's spirit by saying:**
   "I bless your spirit to lead your soul and body."

2. **Before you go to sleep each night, take turns saying this to each other or to yourself:**
   "_____, I call your spirit to come forth to be prominent over your soul and body so that you may receive all the rest and revelation Holy Spirit brings to you through the night... He gives to His beloved even as they sleep."

3. **Every morning when you awake, take turns saying this to each other or to yourself:**
   "_____, I call your spirit to attention to operate in a leadership role over your soul and body. And _____, I call your spirit into alignment with the purpose of Jesus for your life today."

FACE TO FACE BLESSING

1. **Looking face-to-face into each other's eyes, call your spouse's spirit to attention to lead their soul and body.**

2. **Begin speaking positive, biblical truth about what you see in them.**

    For example, "I see _____ in you."

    Give blessings of encouragement. For example, "I bless your spirit to know_____."

    Or, "I bless your spirit to receive _____."

3. **Take turns back and forth for about 5 – 10 times.**

Allow these exercises to be a starting point for nurturing your emotional and spiritual connection. Be creative in trying other applications that you may discover along the way.

SPIRIT BLESSING FOR SINGLES

(Use this to bless other people's spirits as well as your own spirit. You can do this while looking in the mirror or just speaking it out over yourself.)

1. **Look into the other person's eyes, call their spirit to attention to lead their soul and body.**

2. **Listen to Holy Spirit as you begin speaking positive truth about what you see in them.**

    For example, "I see _____ in you."

    Give blessings of encouragement. For example, "I bless your spirit to know_____."

    Or, "I bless your spirit to receive _____."

SPIRIT BLESSING USING SCRIPTURE

A great way to bless your own spirit or another's is to start with a scripture passage that Holy Spirit is highlighting to you and expand on it.

For example, "I bless your spirit 'to know what is the hope of His calling'. I bless you to walk in hope, to find exactly what the Lord is calling you to and to fulfill your calling with joy!"

Or

"I bless you to 'set your mind upon the things above, not on the things that are on Earth'. I bless you to live more aware of Heaven than Earth. I bless you to walk by the Spirit and overcome the flesh. I bless you to overcome the worries of this world."

For more examples, please see Arthur Burk and Sylvia Gunter's book *Blessing Your Spirit*. This book is a wonderful tool to help you become familiar and skilled in this area.

STEPS TO RECONCILIATION

Respond to the following with clear, concise statements and without any explanation or justification for your behavior.

1. This is what I did wrong or this is what I did that hurt you.

2. This is the pain that I believe I put you through because of what I did.

   Ask for feedback:
   - Did I identify and understand the pain you went through?
   - Is there something else that I missed that would be good for me to know?

3. This is how I feel about putting you through that pain.

4. It is my sincere desire, as best as I can, to change this behavior and not bring this pain into your life again.

5. Look at the other person and ask them, "Can you forgive me for this pain I have put you through or this wrong I have done to you?"

Note: If you go through this exercise with empty words and do not follow through with sincere and diligent effort to change, you will only succeed in disappointing your spouse or the other person again and betraying his/her trust in you.

RULES FOR WORKING THROUGH CONFLICT

The following will work well when both parties are actively and willingly working towards understanding each other in a mutually respectful and honest relationship.

1. **Attitude:**

    (a) Approach the discussion with the attitude of, "I don't have to win this argument and I don't have to be the one who is right."

    (b) Make the truth about yourself with respect to the issues and whatever is best for everyone concerned of paramount importance. Take the stance of committing yourselves to following these principles above anything that you feel or fear or desire.

    (c) Humble yourself enough to listen and learn from the person with whom you are in conflict. If you hear a good idea coming from the other person, then validate it!

2. **The first person talks:**

    (a) Approach the discussion with the attitude that, "I don't have to win this argument and I don't have to be the one who is right."

    (b) The first person talks:

    - **Don't** try to cover every aspect of the issue in one communication.
    - **Don't** try to do a "sales job" on the other person.
    - **Do** give reasons why you believe that your ideas or opinions would be the best choice for everyone affected by them.

    (c) The longer you talk, the more complicated the discussion becomes. When many issues are raised at the same time, it can become confusing and overwhelming for the other person to choose which issues to respond to.

    (d) Also the longer you talk without a chance to hear from the other person when in conflict, the more likely you are to hit sensitive issues and stir up hurt, resentment, etc.

3. **Listen:**

    (a) Try to pay more attention to what the other person is saying rather than to what you are going to say in rebuttal.

    (b) Try to hear not only the words but the heart attitudes of the person talking.

4. **The second person talks:**

    (a) The first response should be questions or statements to clarify what you heard, just to be sure you understand correctly before responding.

    (b) The next step is to **state the things that you can agree with** that the first person has said and why you agree with them.

    (c) **Only after these two steps is it okay to give your contrasting or opposing views and the reasons for them.** When giving your opposing views, be sure to follow all of the guidelines listed in #2 above.

5. **Resolution:**

    (a) Continue the four steps above, going back and forth while maintaining the proper attitude. Give time to the process even though it may be tense and seem tedious.

    (b) **Do not** agree to decisions or conclusions that you don't really believe in just to end the conflict, to make the other person feel better, or to try to prevent anger. You must continue talking respectfully and listening until both (or all involved) can come to the place where each can honestly say, "I can live with that," or "I think that would be the best choice for us all."

    (c) Honor your agreements by keeping them until or if a new agreement is made.

    (d) If you do this process well and still cannot come to a consensus, you may need a third party mediator or there may be individual issues that need attention first.

USER-FRIENDLY VERSION

Make sure you have mastered the five steps above before using this shortened, user-friendly version.

1. **Attitude**
   - I don't have to win or be right.
   - Choose what is best for **all** concerned.
   - Choose this above anything you feel, fear or desire.
   - Humble yourself to listen and learn.
   - Validate everything good you hear.

2. **First Person Talks**
   - Be **concise**.
   - Don't **cover** everything.
   - Don't **sell**.
   - Say **why** your idea is valid.

3. **Second Person Listens**
   - Don't just think about a rebuttal.
   - Listen past their words to their heart.

4. **Second Person Talks**
   - **Clarify**.
   - State **agreements**.
   - Share **alternate** views and **why**.

   (Remember to use guidelines from step one.)

5. **Repeat these steps until there is mutual resolution.**

REVEAL YOUR MIND

This exercise is for those who have a difficult time finding things to talk about or those who believe they have nothing to say. It is for the purpose of developing an awareness of internal thoughts and feelings that do not get expressed in words. Ask your spouse or a friend to help you practice this tool.

1. **Take five minutes to pay attention to whatever is going through your mind and speak it out.**

2. **Try to keep talking for five minutes.** Don't worry about changing subjects if your mind wanders. Don't worry if you seem to be rambling, just get used to identifying your thoughts and feelings and putting them into words.

3. **You can't say, "There's nothing on my mind."** As long as you are alive, your mind is active and aware of something. Pay attention and become aware. It is like free association. Use this as an exercise/discipline to help you bring what's on the inside (of you) out.

GODLY GRIEVING

"Blessed are those who mourn, they will be comforted." -Matthew 5:4

1. **Choose one issue, and fully acknowledge your pain and suffering. Don't try to minimize the pain or find a way to "make it go away."**

   Pray: "Father, I give You permission to teach me Godly grieving and take me through this grieving process. Thank You for Your promise that as I mourn, I will be blessed and comforted."

2. **Freely communicate your suffering to the Lord.**

   "Trust in Him at all times, O people; Pour out your heart before Him; God is a refuge for us." -Psalm 62:8

   Activity: Write a letter to God describing how you feel.

3. **Know that He cares about your tears and sorrows. Cry out to the Lord for His help.**

   "He will wipe away every tear from their eyes; and there will no longer be any death; there will no longer be any mourning, or crying or pain; the first things have passed away." -Revelation 21:4

   Activity: Write down the ways you've tried to deal with your pain on your own.

4. **Continue talking to the Lord about your pain and seeking His help until you receive His direction.**

   Activity: Write a letter from God to you and let Him speak to you about how He wants to take you through this process.

5. When He speaks, obey! You must be willing to follow however He directs you.

   "Many are the afflictions of the righteous; but the Lord delivers him out of them all." -Psalms 34:19

Be persistent! Don't stop this process until the Lord delivers you. Repeat this process as necessary, especially with other issues that need grieving.

*For this tool to work well, only go through the Godly Grieving process with one issue at a time.

TOOLS
FOR MARRIED
COUPLES

IDEAS FOR GOING DEEPER

1. Talk about dreams and hopes and the goals needed to achieve them.

2. Talk about your purpose and destiny as a couple in these last days.

3. Talk about any recent spiritual insight you've received.

4. Talk about revelation:
   - What the Lord's speaking personally to you
   - What He's speaking about you
   - What He's speaking to you about your spouse

5. Talk about something you're learning.

6. Share one of your dreams; talk about the interpretation.

7. Review and discuss prophetic words you both have received.

8. Talk about kids/friends/family in a meaningful way:
   - Who are they?
   - What do they need?
   - How are they affecting you and you them?
   - What is God doing in them?
   - Discern how the enemy is coming against them.

9. Talk about how you're feeling (good or bad); find your emotion on the "Feeling Words" chart and talk about it.

10. How are you doing spiritually and emotionally?

11. What are you appreciating about each other? How can you encourage your spouse?

12. Pray together in a meaningful way.

THE 4–2 MAINTENANCE PLAN

Husbands: 4 times per week, for 20 minutes each day, initiate a time to meet and talk with your wife.

Here are some questions that you can start with and then be sure to listen well and respond with interest and understanding:
- How was your day?
- How are you doing emotionally?
- How are you doing spiritually?
- What is one good thing that happened today?
- Was there anything difficult that happened today?
- Did you make a significant connection with anyone today?
- What ways did you think about, feel or connect with God today?
- If you could plan the perfect date for us considering our resources and time commitments, what would it look like?

Your wife really wants to know what's inside of you, so share with her as well:
- What are some things you're really excited about in your life right now that you simply haven't shared with her?
- What are some hard things you're going through?
- Share how you see yourself doing emotionally.
- Share how you feel you are doing spiritually.
- What are some things you'd like God to do for her, for you, for your kids, for your marriage?
- Tell her something that you would really like to do with her on a date.
- Tell her things about your day that you think she would enjoy hearing.

Wives: 2 times per week, pursue your husband sexually.

Here are some suggestions:
- Initiate having sex.
- Make him feel wanted and desired.
- Create a romantic atmosphere with candles or lighting.
- Early in the day, begin preparing yourself mentally and emotionally to give your body as a gift to your husband that night.
- Wear something fun that your husband would like.
- Ask Holy Spirit to help you be creative.

CEREMONY OF LOVING COMMITMENT

(TOGETHER) My dear (spouse's name), as I stand before God and these witnesses, I recommit myself to fulfill my marriage vows to you.
I promise to devote myself to knowing, understanding and loving you more.
I purpose to pursue knowing God's love and affection for me, walking obediently with Him, and loving Him above anything or anyone else; so that I can become the person that God desires me to be for you.

(MEN) I purpose anew to cherish and love you and lay down my life for you as Christ laid down His life for the church.
I commit myself to join with the Holy Spirit on your behalf to encourage you into a place of maturity and wholeness in Christ; that will allow us to walk in the destiny God has planned for us.

(WOMEN) I purpose anew to respect and honor you as the protector and covering that God has called you to be over this home.
I commit myself to join with the Holy Spirit to affirm, support, love and encourage you towards your Godly role as the spiritual head of our home.

(TOGETHER) I choose to make you and our marriage relationship a priority over any other human relationship.
I promise to continue to move towards living with you in a truthful, honest and vulnerable way, withholding nothing of significance, concealing nothing of importance.
I will honor you by taking the initiative to share things with you about my life and about us that would be important to you, to God and the well-being of our family.
I commit to not settling but consistently going farther, deeper and higher in our relationship with one another so that my heart will be fully turned towards you, so that the world will see Jesus' love in us and in our family.

NOTES

NOTES

NOTES

NOTES